Rooster Chinese Horoscope 2025

By

IChingHunFùyǒu FengShuisu

Table of Contents

Introduce

The character of people born in the year of the ROOSTER

People born this year are sincere to others and always care about others. When you see others in danger, you are quick to help, are always enthusiastic, and like to talk. For this reason, people born this year have quite a lot of friends and also have a habit of dressing up nicely. But most of them are on sale. People born this year do not like anything extravagant.

People born this year are always careful with themselves and can solve problems well, suitable for the professions of doctors, detectives, psychologists, and nurses. People born this year are people who are not still. In addition, the skills that are available in many In your honesty, you'll be a devoted friend. When the year of the rooster falls in love with you, you are ready to give up your life and do whatever you love.

Strength:
You have a strong sense of self and enjoy drawing attention to yourself.

Weaknesses:
You enjoy interfering in other people's affairs and, at times, irritate others without even realizing it.

Love:
People born this year are flirting, not telling anyone, and never leaving love. When you love someone, you will pay more attention to them and take better care of them. You have one distinguishing feature: you never forget to stop by or purchase a personalized gift for a loved one. You're always adding a splash of color to your love life, whether it's outside, inside, or even in bed. For people born in the year of the Rooster, infidelity or sharing love with others is almost unavoidable. It is important to exercise caution when it comes to love. If you get a boyfriend who doesn't understand each other and ignores the small details, it may unintentionally turn into a big story.

Suitable Career:

Those born in the Year of the Rooster are those born in the golden element. As a result, a suitable job or occupation is frequently one that requires the use of talent. As well as their originality architects, artists, songwriters, singers, actors, models, models, car sales, industrial plants, steel bar sales, steel production, pile making, car parts, jewelry shops, jewelry making or gold shops, and so on. They are all appropriate occupations for people born in the year of the Rooster.

Year of the ROOSTER (Water) | (1945) & (2005)

"The Rooster in the Coop" is a person born in the year of the ROOSTER at the age of 80 years (1945) and 20 years (2005)

Overview

For senior horoscopes in this age group, since this year auspicious stars are shining brightly, which are stars that will make you progress in your career and business, all the irregularities in the past year will gradually disappear, so you won't have many problems to worry about this year. The only thing you should be careful about is that you have to take good care of your health. If you are traveling outside or on a long trip, you should have your children take care of you for safety. In addition, inauspicious stars are staring at you in your horoscope house, which will make you moody and irritable. Therefore, you should control your emotions and conduct yourself well this year. You should not interfere in your children's and grandchildren's matters because knowing too much will only make you stressed. It is better to focus on taking care of your health.

For young horoscopes, this year there will be a lonely energy around you, making you want to be alone and isolated from society, not wanting to socialize with anyone much. In many work activities, whether it is education or work, you should increase your patience and diligence. In any case, you must always develop new skills. Do not stop seeking knowledge and developing yourself. Even if there are obstacles along the way, do not be discouraged because along the way you will find someone to help you. Please keep your determination. Things you should be mindful of this year: even if you feel irritated, you need to keep your feelings to yourself. Venting your emotions on others, whether friends or people close to you, sometimes may not be intentional or may be seen as a joke, but with some matters and some people, this is the beginning of a vengeful account waiting to be paid. And be careful of people close to you who will betray you and cause you shame and pain. For the love aspect of this person, this year there will be both good and bad things mixed. Be careful of a third party and arguments in your love life.

Career and Business

This year, you will see progress whether it is in business, work, or education. It will tend to be positive. Please be determined and always improve your skills to keep up with the current situation. The results will be worth the hard work, especially during the months when your work and education have good progress, namely the 4th Chinese month (May 5 – June 4), the 6th Chinese month (July 7 – August 6), the 7th Chinese month (August 7 – September 6), and the 9th Chinese month (October 8 – November 6). During these periods, starting a new job, entering into joint ventures, and investing can proceed according to the plan. But you should be careful during the following months when your work and education will encounter obstacles and problems, which are the 2nd Chinese month (March 5 - April 3), the 3rd Chinese month (April 4 - May 4), the 8th Chinese month (September 7 - October 7), and the 11th Chinese month (7 December 7, 2025 - 4 January 4, 2026). You should be careful about making contracts and making work connections that may cause problems. Also, be careful of being bullied and jealous of people who may try to harass you. You should also avoid making investments because there is a high chance of suffering damages and losses.

Financial

This year, the financial horoscope of both horoscopes is considered quite good. The senior horoscope can find children or reliable assistants to take care of the investment. If combined with your experience, you will be able to make profits as targeted. Especially in the following months, your finances will flow smoothly: 4th Chinese month (May 5 - June 4), 6th Chinese month (July 7 - August 6), 7th Chinese month (August 7 - September 6), and Chinese 9th month (October 8 - November 6). However, you should not be careful during the period of financial problems and unexpected expenses in the following months: the 2nd Chinese month (March 5 - April 3), the 3rd Chinese month (April 4 - May 4), the 8th Chinese month (September 7 - October 7), and 11th Chinese month (December 7, 2025 - January 4, 2026), when you should not gamble or take risks. Do not lend money to others or sign as a financial guarantee. Do not be greedy for ill-gotten gains or greedy for the benefits that others bring to tempt you. Be careful not to fall victim to fraud.

Family

The family horoscope of both horoscopes this year will find auspicious power. There will be an important guest visiting the house. During the year, there will be an opportunity to organize an auspicious event or receive good news about the success of family members. For the elderly, there will be a birthday party (Saik), gathering relatives to congratulate and create joy at home. It is a good thing. However, you should be careful during the months that are not supportive and there will be problems and chaos in your family, which are the 2nd Chinese month (March 5 - April 3), the 3rd Chinese month (April 4 - May 4), the 8th Chinese month (September 7 - October 7), and the 11th Chinese month (December 7, 2025 - January 4, 2026). Be careful of accidents from scammers that may happen to family members.

Be careful of juniors or servants causing trouble and damage. In addition, be careful of being betrayed, slandered, and slandered by ill-wishers. Be careful of words that may unintentionally make the other person unhappy. It will create resentment and wait for revenge. And you shouldn't get involved in your friends' conflicts.

Love

For senior people this year, you must be careful not to use emotions and not to interfere in the matters of your children and grandchildren. This will make the relationship in the family with your children and grandchildren smooth and respect you well. For young people, love this year is not stable. Therefore, in matters of love and heart, you must not be hasty. If you love someone, do not be too passionate because you are still young and have a lot of time to find the right person for you. For those who have a lover, be careful not to be too hasty because you may regret it later. The months when your love is quite fragile and there will be reasons to be upset easily are the 2nd Chinese month (March

5 - April 3), the 3rd Chinese month (April 4 - May 4), the 8th Chinese month (September 7 - October 7), and the 11th Chinese month (December 7, 2025 - January 4, 2026). You must be careful when talking to the opposite sex because it can easily cause arguments. Be careful of a third party interfering and undermining the relationship. Also, you should not interfere in other people's family matters or go to entertainment venues. Be careful not to catch a serious disease.

Health

For senior people, there is a chance of being sick and recovering. Therefore, you should get enough rest, do light exercise, and strictly take care of your diet. For young people, you should be careful about the hygiene of your food and drinking. Avoid things that undermine your health because they will cause you to lose money, especially during the 2nd Chinese month (March 5 – April 3), 3rd Chinese month (April 4 – May 4), 8th Chinese month (September 7 – October 7), and 11th Chinese month (December 7, 2025 – January 4, 2026).

During these periods, you must be careful of accidents while working and traveling both near and far. You should also be careful of other unexpected dangers. In addition, you must be careful of getting sick, especially for senior people. Be careful of slipping and falling and unexpected complications. Therefore, you should avoid visiting sick people at night. You should also avoid attending funeral rites and eating at the funeral.

Year of the ROOSTER (Fire) | (1957) (2017)

"An Independent ROOSTER." is a person born in the year of the ROOSTER at the age of 68 years (1957) and 8 years (2017)

Overview

For the senior horoscope of this year, even though inauspicious stars are staring and disturbing you in your horoscope house, you will be able to get through this because there are auspicious stars to help you. However, because of the influence of the evil stars, you will be isolated. There will be fewer people visiting you, to the point that you may feel lonely and disappointed that your children have abandoned you. You should also be careful with words that may hurt the feelings of those close to you without realizing it. Therefore, you shouldn't interfere in other people's matters or accidentally criticize the lives of your children and grandchildren for your peace. In addition, what you should be careful about is health problems, especially food and diet, which you must control the amount of sugar and fat, avoid alcoholic drinks, and spend economically, which will help you have liquidity. In addition, you should be careful of problems in your relationships with your neighbors because there will be conflicts that will lead to disasters and troubles. In life, we should not use strength to bully anyone because winning with force is not a true victory. If you can win over others with goodness, it will be a good and permanent victory.

For young horoscopes, this year there are auspicious stars in orbit, which will result in progress in studies. Therefore, please be diligent in your studies and divide your time between playing and studying well.

Then you will be successful and will be admired and loved by adults and teachers. Things to be careful of are infectious diseases that come from eating food carelessly and the dangers of injury from doing various activities. In addition, parents should be more careful of dangers related to water, whether it is water tourism, traveling, water transportation, or playing water sports. You should be careful of encountering dangers from accidents from playing carelessly.

Career and Business

For seniors, in terms of work and trade, even though the overall picture looks smooth, there will be conflicts among individuals in the organization and they will have to constantly solve nagging problems during work throughout the year. However, if a problem occurs, you should quickly resolve it before it escalates and causes damage, especially during the months when work will encounter obstacles, namely the 2nd Chinese month (March 5 – April 3), the 3rd Chinese month (April 4 – May 4), the 8th Chinese month (September 7 – October 7), and the 11th Chinese month (December 7, 2025 – January 4, 2026). When working, accepting work, or giving orders, you should communicate clearly to prevent mistakes from occurring. You should also explain the advantages and disadvantages to the other party in detail so that there are options. This is because everything has both advantages and disadvantages. However, this year is a good time for you to look for heirs or children to help continue the work, especially to take care of adjustments, improvements, and expansions. Combining modern and old ideas and perspectives will help many things work together and achieve better results according to the goals. The months when work and investment will be smooth are the 4th Chinese month (May 5 – June 4), the 6th Chinese month (July 7 – August 6), the 7th Chinese month (August 7 – September 6), and the 9th Chinese month (October 8 – November 6).

Financial

Although this year's overall financial fortune is good, there will be unexpected expenses that will drain your liquidity, leading to a crisis of financial instability at some point. Therefore, what can help is saving and spending only on necessities, which will help you have some liquidity left to spend in an emergency. The months when your finances will be stuck and unexpected expenses will occur are the 2nd Chinese month (March 5 - April 3), the 3rd Chinese month (April 4 - May 4), the 8th Chinese month (September 7 - October 7), and the 11th Chinese month (December 7, 2025 - January 4, 2026). You should not gamble, lend money to others, or be a financial guarantor. You should not be greedy for wealth that does not belong to you. Be careful of falling victim to fraud, and do not invest in illegal or immoral businesses. The months when financial fortune is liquid are the 4th Chinese month (May 5 – June 4), the 6th Chinese month (July 7 – August 6), the 7th Chinese month (August 7 – September 6), and the 9th Chinese month (October 8 – November 6).

Family

This year, your family destiny lacks peace because inauspicious stars are moving into your zodiac house to disturb you. Therefore, during the year, you will not be able to avoid chaos in your home. In particular, you must be careful of unexpected accidents that may cause injuries. You must also be careful about your safety and property, arguments in your home, and problems with your neighbors. You should also be careful not to be too strong and bully those who are weaker. Bullying others will lead to revenge later. Therefore, it is better to make friends rather than make enemies. In particular, the months when you must be careful of problems and chaos in your family are the 2nd Chinese month (March 5 – April 3), the 3rd Chinese month (April 4 – May 4), the 8th Chinese month (September 7 – October 7), and the 11th Chinese month (December 7, 2025 – January 4, 2026). In addition, you should frequently check the fixtures and equipment installed in your home because they may fall and harm people in the home. Electrical appliances, tools, and sharp objects should be kept in good condition and used with caution. To avoid damage and loss, you must be careful of losing valuables and property, and be careful of people in the house falling victim to fraudsters. In addition, you should not get involved in conflicts between friends. During this time, children should not go out to play in the water with friends. Be careful of various dangers from the water.

Love

This year, the love horoscope of the senior horoscope is considered quite good. You will have the opportunity to travel with your partner both in Thailand and abroad. You will also have the opportunity to work or host a merit-making event or a social welfare event. You will receive pampering and care from your partner, making you happy throughout the year. As for the young horoscope, some people love and support you. However, parents should teach children of this age to speak politely, and not to be loud or aggressive. Instead, they should respect adults, know how to share and be kind to friends, and help family members with their work as much as possible. This will make children of this age lovable and more loved by those close to them. For the months when the love of the elders is rather fragile and may easily cause arguments, they are the 2nd Chinese month (March 5 – April 3), the 3rd Chinese month (April 4 – May 4), the 8th Chinese month (September 7 – October 7), and the 11th Chinese month (December 7, 2025 – January 4, 2026). Avoid the cause of arguments and do not get involved with other couples.

Health

This year, the health of the elderly is not good. You tend to be irritated and moody easily. Some things that are not important should be let go, otherwise, it will hurt your health. It is best to get enough rest and not stress about your children too much. In terms of illnesses, you should be careful of gastritis, liver disease, and silent diseases that may show symptoms. Please observe yourself often. If you feel insomnia, or stress, have no appetite, abnormal bowel movements, or any part of your body is swollen or sore, see a doctor for diagnosis and treatment. Early diagnosis and treatment will help ease the burden. The months when you should closely monitor your health are the 2nd Chinese month (March 5 - April 3), the 3rd Chinese month (April 4 - May 4), the 8th Chinese month (September 7 - October 7), and the 11th Chinese month (December 7, 2025 - January 4, 2026). In addition to being more careful about health problems, you should also be more careful about injuries from accidents and falls. For children, during this period, be more careful about injuries from accidents and dangers from water.

Year of the ROOSTER (Earth) | (1969)

" The Rooster during the autumn season " is a person born in the year of the ROOSTER at the age of 56 years (1969)

Overview

For the person born in the year of the Rakarn, this year is considered an auspicious year for you, resulting in your career progress. Those who are doing business will flourish and have a smooth life. Investments will have positive results. However, you should maintain diligence and perseverance and constantly develop new skills for yourself. This will help your career to be more prosperous. No matter what you think or do this year, you will receive good support and assistance from people who will support you along the way. However, since during this year, there will be an evil star moving into your horoscope house, it will result in accidents and unexpected health effects. In particular, you should be careful of gastritis, intestinal diseases, diabetes, liver disease, high blood pressure, and silent internal diseases that may flare up and show symptoms. Therefore, you should take care of your health more strictly and closely. You should also find opportunities to make merit by going to make merit at monks' hospitals or donating blood, body, or money to hospitals to ward off bad luck related to illness and health. If you want to improve your career and finances, you should find time to practice Vipassana meditation or help with charitable activities to achieve success. It will help increase and enhance your reputation in your career and business even more.

Career and Business

This year is another year in which your career has a path of progress. You will find a patron and support from friends and business partners. Therefore, it is a good time to increase sales, expand production bases, expand branches, launch products or open new markets, and increase investment in new businesses. If you can find heirs or assistants to help continue the work, it will make the investment more successful. Especially during the months when the owner's career and business have a good direction of progress and prosperity, namely the 4th Chinese month (May 5 - June 4), the 6th Chinese month (July 7 - August 6), the 7th Chinese month (August 7 - September 6), and the 9th Chinese month (October 8 - November 6). However, you should be careful of subordinates or followers who make mistakes and cause damage. Therefore, when giving orders, there should be clear communication and instructions on the points that should be taken care of to reduce mistakes. In addition, the legal procedures for various contracts You should be especially careful during the following months when your work and trade will easily encounter obstacles, problems, and mistakes, namely the 2nd Chinese month (March 5 - April 3), the 3rd Chinese month (April 4 - May 4), the 8th Chinese month (September 7 - October 7) and the 11th Chinese month (December 7, 2025 - January 4, 2026). You should also avoid investing during these periods.

Financial

This year, the fortuneteller's finances will fluctuate. Income and expenses are still uncertain. They may encounter unexpected current expenses or unexpected financial leakages. Therefore, the first easy solution is to spend wisely, only spend on necessities, and save up. Although it may not reduce expenses, it will help you smile when disaster strikes. In particular, the months when you need to be careful and prepare for financial problems are the 2nd Chinese month (March 5 - April 3), the 3rd Chinese month (April 4 - May 4), the 8th Chinese month (September 7 - October 7), and the 11th Chinese month (December 7, 2025 - January 4, 2026). In addition, gambling is prohibited. Lending money or signing financial guarantees is prohibited. Greed for wealth that does not belong to you and investment in illegal or immoral businesses is prohibited. The months when your finances will return to flowing smoothly are the 4th Chinese month (May 5 – June 4), the 6th Chinese month (July 7 – August 6), the 7th Chinese month (August 7 – September 6), and the 9th Chinese month (October 8 – November 6).

Family

This year, the family events of this person are not good because they are influenced by the evil stars. Therefore, you must be prepared to be careful of unexpected dangers or old and damaged fixtures that may fall and harm the people in the house. Therefore, you should always check which fixtures are old and which electrical appliances are damaged or close to being damaged. You should quickly repair or replace them for safety. You should also be careful of the health problems of the people in the house. However, if you have the opportunity to organize any auspicious events in your house, it will help to reduce the inauspicious energy. Or you can buy expensive items that you like from the beginning of the year to solve the bad luck of losing money. This will help to some extent. However, you should be more careful during the following months when there is a chance of conflict in the family, which are the 2nd Chinese month (March 5 - April 3), the 3rd Chinese month (April 4 - May 4), the 8th Chinese month (September 7 - October 7), and the 11th Chinese month (December 7, 2025 - January 4, 2026). Be more careful of accidents. Be careful of subordinates or servants causing trouble. Be careful of valuables being damaged, lost, or falling victim to fraud. Also, do not get involved in conflicts between friends, especially those that lead to legal cases.

Love

This year, love is full of ups and downs. There will be frequent arguments, especially in the following months when your love will be fragile and conflicts will easily arise: the 2nd Chinese month (March 5 – April 3), the 3rd Chinese month (April 4 – May 4), the 8th Chinese month (September 7 – October 7), and the 11th Chinese month (December 7, 2025 – January 4, 2026). Therefore, please try to avoid arguing. Be calm and patient. When the storm passes, peace will return. Be firm and do not listen to criticism and gossip. You should control your behavior and avoid going to entertainment venues that will bring chaos.

Health

The health of the person must not be careless. Although your health is generally good, in your horoscope, due to the impact of the celestial stars that are disturbing and disturbing, you must be careful of hidden illnesses. Therefore, you should observe for abnormal symptoms in your body and should go for regular check-ups. Because if you enter a month that is not favorable to you, which is the 2nd Chinese month (March 5 - April 3), the 3rd Chinese month (April 4 - May 4), the 8th Chinese month (September 7 - October 7), and the 11th Chinese month (December 7, 2025 - January 4, 2026), there will be old and new health problems or silent threats. Therefore, you should reduce going out at night, including going to entertainment venues and reduce drinking alcoholic beverages, which are not good for your health, especially liver disease and other hidden diseases.

In addition, you should pay more attention to the hygiene of your food and drink, and be careful of stomach diseases, intestinal diseases, heart disease, and abnormal blood pressure. Avoid visiting sick people at night and avoid attending funerals. Be extra careful about accidents both while working and traveling.

Year of the ROOSTER (Wood) | (1981)

" The Rooster in the Coop" is a person born in the year of the ROOSTER at the age of 44 years (1981)

Overview

For the person born in the year of the Rakarn, this year is another year that you should be brave in making decisions to achieve prosperity. Your career will experience a path of progress. Businesses will have the opportunity to expand, and increase sales and income, or investments will yield satisfactory returns. Therefore, it is considered a good year for some people who are thinking of starting a business because they will have the power to support them in establishing and having their own business. For those who are already running a business, there is an opportunity to expand their work, add branches, or buy or invest in new businesses. There will be an opportunity to buy expensive property. There will be an auspicious time to move into a new place of work. However, during the year, many bad stars appear in the horoscope house, which all affect your life. This causes you to be moody, irritated, and easily irritated. If someone says something unpleasant, you will often respond with harsh words that displease those around you without you knowing. This makes those around you not want to be friends with you and may not cooperate in your work. In addition, sometimes you will feel bored and not want to meet, talk, or socialize with anyone. You want to be alone. You will feel annoyed by everything you encounter, easily get angry, and be hot-tempered, which will result in accidents and health problems. Conflicts at work often cause headaches. Accumulate stress and become annoyed. Therefore, the first solution is that you should know how to divide time between work and personal matters. You should set time for yourself to get enough sleep. Even though you are a healthy working person, your body has flesh and blood, not a machine. You should have some time for maintenance. The second is to know how to control your emotions. If you are angry at someone, do not immediately take it out on them because that is not the right way to solve the problem. You should be kind to people around you. Then your chances of advancement will be within reach.

Career and Business

This year, your business will experience prosperity. There are criteria for finding supporters to help you, so you have the opportunity to expand your work, expand your branches, or expand your investment. Therefore, you should increase your diligence, and always improve your skills and knowledge, to keep up with the changing situations around you. Use your knowledge, experience, and resources to the fullest to create progress, create visible results, or take your business to the next level. Especially during the months when your business will flourish, namely the 4th Chinese month (May 5 – June 4), the 6th Chinese month (July 7 – August 6), the 7th Chinese month (August 7 – September 6), and the 9th Chinese month (October 8 – November 6). In addition, this year, you must consider starting a new job, entering into a joint venture, and investing in various areas. Do not be hasty in accepting invitations, because the inviter will only talk about the positive side and not the negative side. If you see that investing will result in negative results, you should know how to refuse without fear of losing face or hurting each other's feelings. In particular, the following months when careers tend to decline and obstacles often occur are the 2nd Chinese month (March 5 – April 3), the 3rd Chinese month (April 4 – May 4), the 8th Chinese month (September 7 – October 7), and the 11th Chinese month (December 7, 2025 – January 4, 2026). Be careful of falling into investment traps that cause damage and loss of property. Also, be careful of making long-term binding contracts that will cause problems later on. Also, be careful of insiders who are worms or you may encounter accounting fraud during the months that do not support you as mentioned above.

Financial

Your financial horoscope this year is quite good. Income will flow in from two sources: income from salary or sales, as well as extra income from windfalls. Therefore, please increase your diligence, keep developing new skills, and quickly move forward to seize opportunities. There will be an opportunity to advance to another level. In particular, the months when finances flow smoothly are the 4th Chinese month (May 5 - June 4), the 6th Chinese month (July 7 - August 6), the 7th Chinese month (August 7 - September 6), and the 9th Chinese month (October 8 - November 6).

However, be careful of the months when your finances will be stuck and unexpected expenses will occur, namely the 2nd Chinese month (March 5 - April 3), the 3rd Chinese month (April 4 - May 4), the 8th Chinese month (September 7 - October 7), and the 11th Chinese month (December 7, 2025 - January 4, 2026), when you should not lend money or sign financial guarantees, gamble, or take risks, and do not do illegal or immoral businesses.

Family

This year, your family will be happy. You will have good luck or good news. You will have the opportunity to buy expensive property. There will be an auspicious time to move into a new house. In addition, you will find support from elders. You will also receive advice and methods to solve crises in your work from relatives. However, you should be careful during the months when problems and chaos will occur in your family, which are the 2nd Chinese month (March 5 - April 3), the 3rd Chinese month (April 4 - May 4), the 8th Chinese month (September 7 - October 7), and the 11th Chinese month (December 7, 2025 - January 4, 2026). During these periods, be careful of people in the house arguing with neighbors. Be careful of old and damaged electrical appliances or things that are attached to the house falling and causing harm. Be careful of valuables that are damaged, lost, or falling victim to fraud. Also, do not get involved in conflicts between friends because the other party may misunderstand, which may cause accidents, being attacked, or being slandered and causing damage.

Love

Due to the influence of the lone star, you will often have mood swings and speak in a way that is not considerate. This may cause your love to break up. Therefore, you should be careful to control your words and behavior. Do not show aggression or hurt others. Also, because you have a lot of work, you may not have time to care for those around you. Sometimes, indifference may make the other person suspicious. Therefore, do not forget to set aside time to take care of those at home. Also, a third party may appear to create a rift and make your relationship unstable. In particular, you should be careful during the 2nd Chinese month (March 5 – April 3), 3rd Chinese month (April 4 – May 4), 8th Chinese month (September 7 – October 7), and 11th Chinese month (December 7, 2025 – January 4, 2026). You should not get involved with other people's spouses and avoid going to entertainment venues.

Health

This year, the health of the person is in the middle range. You should divide your work and rest time appropriately. Increase your attention to hygiene in drinking and eating. Beware of food poisoning, including food that is too sweet, greasy, salty, and food that will increase the body's heat, such as grilled, fried, and roasted food, which will cause internal heat, so you should avoid it. Especially in the following months, you need to pay extra attention to your health, which are the 2nd Chinese month (March 5 - April 3), the 3rd Chinese month (April 4 - May 4), the 8th Chinese month (September 7 - October 7), and the 11th Chinese month (December 7, 2025 - January 4, 2026). Beware of illness, dizziness, and accidents while working and using the road.

Year of the ROOSTER (Golden) | (1993)

" The rooster crows in the morning" is a person born in the year of the ROOSTER at the age of 32 years (1993)

Overview

For young people born in the year of the Rooster, this year is another year that will bring auspicious power. Whatever you think or do, you will find a patron to support you. As a result, you will be successful in both your career and finances. Whether you expand your business or invest in business, everything will go well. Therefore, if you know how to use your existing intelligence, along with determination and diligence to develop new skills, you will be able to create good and abundant work. The good deeds and abilities you have done this year will not be lost. Your elders and superiors will be fond of you and trust you, giving you higher positions and responsibilities, which is career advancement.

In addition, auspicious stars also promote the power of self-establishment, meaning that you will be able to have your own business, have the opportunity to expand your business, invest in your favorite business, acquire a business, or become a partner in your dream business. When the heavens open up, opportunities for luck await you. You must be determined and brave enough to take action, because there is support from all around, plus problems and obstacles that will arise will be less, because auspicious stars help support and promote many things to be completed easily.

This year is a good opportunity for you. Don't let it pass you by without doing anything. However, before you start doing anything, you should plan to set clear and careful goals. You also need to consider many factors, from personnel and methods. In particular, human relations skills are very important in both your work and business. Try to build good relationships with people around you so that you will receive good support. During the year, there will be a storm. Please do not be discouraged. Encourage your spirit to keep fighting. Having good morale and strength will help you overcome obstacles. In addition, you must learn to develop yourself to keep up with the changes that often occur. What you hope for will not be disappointed.

Career and Business

Your career this year is a path of prosperity. Your career will progress. Your business will have the opportunity to grow. What is indispensable is diligence and self-development. You should strike while the fire is hot during the months when your career has the power to support and lead in a prosperous direction, namely the 4th Chinese month (May 5 - June 4), the 6th Chinese month (July 7 - August 6), the 7th Chinese month (August 7 - September 6), and the 9th Chinese month (October 8 - November 6). Furthermore, this year is suitable for starting a new job, entering into joint ventures, and investing in various channels. Therefore, you will often have good opportunities to visit you. If you choose the right investment at the right time, you will receive a beautiful return. However, this year, you should be careful about signing work contracts. You should consider the details carefully so that there will be no problems later. In particular, the months when work and business will encounter obstacles and problems are the 2nd Chinese month (March 5 – April 3), the 3rd Chinese month (April 4 – May 4), the 8th Chinese month (September 7 – October 7) and the 11th Chinese month (December 7, 2025 – January 4, 2026) in which you must be careful in business negotiations or work contacts. Try not to interfere or meddle in other people's matters. In addition, during the aforementioned months, starting a new job, entering into a joint venture, and investing in various channels will encounter obstacles. There is a possibility of being tricked and taken advantage of, or unexpected changes in the market may occur, causing damage. Therefore, it should be avoided.

Financial

This year, your financial horoscope is quite good. You will have direct income from salary, sales, profits from trading, extra money from special jobs, commissions, bonuses, and some money from luck. Diligence that comes with new skills will help you have more money. However, if it is during the 2nd Chinese month (March 5 – April 3), 3rd Chinese month (April 4 – May 4), 8th Chinese month (September 7 – October 7), and 11th Chinese month (December 7, 2025 – January 4, 2026), you should not lend money to anyone because there is a chance that you will not get it back. Do not guarantee and should refrain from gambling or taking risks. It will not be worth the loss. If you are thinking of investing in a business this year, you should avoid doing business that is likely to be against the law or copyright infringement because it will cause you trouble and lead to more serious problems. However, this year there are months when finances will flow smoothly and there will be unexpected windfalls, namely the 4th Chinese month (May 5 – June 4), the 6th Chinese month (July 7 – August 6), the 7th Chinese month (August 7 – September 6), and the 9th Chinese month(October 8 – November 6).

Family

Within the family of the person, everything will be smooth. There will be good news or auspicious events. There will also be an opportunity to welcome new members. There will be an opportunity to buy expensive property. There will be an auspicious time to move into a new house and enter a new workplace. In addition, there will be good friends who will be consultants and provide support. There will also be an opportunity to travel together to observe or study work both domestically and internationally. However, you should be careful during the months when your family will experience problems and chaos, namely the 2nd Chinese month (March 5 - April 3), the 3rd Chinese month (April 4 - May 4), the 8th Chinese month (September 7 - October 7), and the 11th Chinese month (December 7, 2025 - January 4, 2026). You must be careful about safety in the home and take care of the elderly in the home closely. Be careful of accidents or unexpected events that may cause loss of property. Be careful of problems of arguments both inside and outside the home.

Be careful of valuables being damaged, lost, or falling victim to scammers. In addition, you should not get involved in conflicts between friends. As for making new friends, you should be careful in choosing who to be with because there is a chance that you will be deceived.

Love

For the love of this year, the person will fall into the trap of charm (Peach trap) which will cause you to easily become infatuated with vices or women. However, this year, your behavior with the opposite sex must be appropriate. Who is your partner, who is your lover, and who is your friend or acquaintance? Dating and talking is normal. Providing assistance and services should be done suitably. Because if you are too close, your lover or partner will not be happy. Also, being charmed by service girls should be careful because it will cause endless worries. Especially during the months when your love is quite fragile and arguments can easily occur, namely the 2nd Chinese month (March 5 - April 3), the 3rd Chinese month (April 4 - May 4), the 8th Chinese month (September 7 - October 7), and the 11th Chinese month (December 7, 2025 - January 4, 2026), you should be careful of slanderous words from people with bad intentions. It will cause misunderstandings between you and your lover. You also need to be careful with your words. Do not use impulse judgment because it will cause more problems. Also, avoid getting involved in other people's couples. Avoid entertainment venues that sell services. Be careful of catching diseases.

Health

This year, the health of the person is generally quite strong. Although you are still young and full of energy, during the year, you will encounter a bad star that is moving to look after your health, which often results in silent disasters or accidents in dark places. Therefore, in the middle of the night, you should be careful because there may be unexpected disasters. Especially in the following months, you should be extra careful and take enough rest: the 2nd Chinese month (March 5 - April 3), the 3rd Chinese month (April 4 - May 4), the 8th Chinese month (September 7 - October 7), and the 11th Chinese month (December 7, 2025 - January 4, 2026). During these times, you should be extra careful of accidents, especially when working or traveling at night. Also, when working with tools, machines, or electrical equipment, you should work under sufficient lighting. And do not be careless, which will help reduce disasters.

Chinese Astrology Horoscope for Each Month

Month 12 in the Dragon Year (5 Jan 25 - 2 Feb 25)
This month, your finances are in a state of ups and downs. There is no certainty. Be careful of

money leakage. Therefore, you should avoid gambling and not lend money to anyone. Do not be a guarantor. Do not do illegal business. Unexpected events will erode your money and affect your liquidity.

In terms of work, there will be conflicts and unrest in the organization. Take good care of your customers and those you have to contact. Be careful of competitors who will come to snatch your good opportunities. Therefore, what you should do this month is to strengthen your relationships with the people around you. Work hard to create more work and increase your income to compensate for the shortfall or damage. Do not isolate yourself from society or you will be forgotten or rejected.

This month, you need to save and tighten your belt. When it comes to spending, choose only necessary things. Save often and plan your finances from the beginning of the month to maintain liquidity throughout the month. When signing contracts this month, you need to look carefully before signing. You should refrain from investing if you do not want to regret it later.

For your family horoscope this month, be careful of the elderly in the house getting sick. Be careful of accidents and stray bullets that will affect you. Also, be careful of juniors causing trouble.

In terms of love, be careful of a third party causing chaos in your relationship. You should be calm, not gullible, be firm, and use cold water to comfort you. Don't let your emotions take the lead, otherwise, the love you have built will be ruined overnight. In addition, you should avoid going to entertainment venues.

In terms of health, be careful of allergies, food poisoning, and other infectious diseases. Be careful of accidents while traveling.

Support Days: 4 Jan., 8 Jan., 12 Jan., 16 Jan., 20 Jan., 24 Jan., 28 Jan.
Lucky Days: 11 Jan., 23 Jan.
Misfortune Days: 10 Jan.,22 Jan.

Bad Days: 5 Jan., 7 Jan., 17 Jan., 19 Jan., 29 Jan., 31 Jan.

Month 1 in the Snake Year (3 Feb 25 - 4 Mar 25)
This month is considered an auspicious month for you. A good start is considered half the success. Therefore, you do not have to worry about past mistakes that will hinder your bright future. You should learn from past mistakes and not repeat them. Also, please remember that "Those who have never done anything wrong are those who have never done anything." Your career and salary are looking bright. Even though there are obstacles, you will be able to overcome them because you have received support and help.

Therefore, what you should do during this period is to plan your long-term work by setting clear goals. Seize good opportunities during this period and move forward. Work to achieve your goals. As for new investments or business expansion, you should plan and prepare your personnel, location, and working capital, and consider the time it will take to get your investment back. In addition, you should assign tasks to your subordinates or subordinates so that they can work on what they are good at. You must have a clear position and follow the plan that you have set to be consistent with your goals. Your financial luck this month is quite good. You will still have a normal income flowing in. However, if you are greedy in gambling, it will lead to poverty.

Your family will be peaceful. If there are obstacles, you will find a patron to help you.

In terms of love, it is time to go on a trip together. Or go to make merit or worship the Buddha to enhance the auspiciousness of yourself and your family.

In terms of health, it is fair. During this time, be careful of stomach diseases, heart disease, and intestinal diseases. Do not eat hot food cooked by grilling, roasting, or frying. You should also be more careful of accidents while traveling.

Support Days: 1 Feb., 5 Feb., 9 Feb., 13 Feb., 17 Feb., 21 Feb., 25 Feb.
Lucky Days: 4 Feb., 16 Feb., 28 Feb.
Misfortune Days: 3 Feb., 15 Feb., 27 Feb.
Bad Days: 10 Feb., 12 Feb., 22 Feb., 24 Feb.

Month 2 in the Snake Year (5 Mar 25 - 3 Apr 25)
Your life path this month has turned downward because evil stars are disturbing your horoscope house. Unexpected events will occur. Therefore, you should be more careful in all activities. You should be careful with your words and control your actions, especially because you may be bullied and attacked by envious people. Do not act arrogantly or you may be disliked.

In terms of work and business, this period will face storms. You will encounter conflicts both internally and externally. Be careful of disputes with customers or business partners that can become a big problem. What you should do is build and strengthen good relationships with people you have to contact all the time to form a network and be able to help and rely on each other in the future. In addition, you must be mindful and calm. Every activity that you will do must be thought carefully and carefully before doing it. Then you will be able to get through it. However, your work during this period may be affected by the liquidity problem. Therefore, you should allocate cash flow or invest and save. If you have income, do not spend it carelessly. You should always keep a record of your income and expenses. Do not be careless.

Your fortune and finances are not good. You will encounter unexpected expenses that will cause you to lose your wealth. If you want to take risks, invest, or test your luck, you should take small risks so that you do not fall into a financial crisis and make it worse. As for working or investing in stocks, you should postpone it for now.

In terms of family, you will find arguments. Be careful of subordinates or servants in the house causing trouble. For relatives and friends, you should distance yourself from friends who like to invite you to hang out.

In terms of love, it is quite shaky. There are often disagreements every day. You should be careful of your behavior and words that hurt others without realizing it. You should not go to entertainment venues.

In terms of health, even though you are strong, you still have to be careful of injuries to the head and chest from accidents.

Support Days: 1 Mar, 5 Mar., 9 Mar., 13 Mar., 17 Mar., 21 Mar., 25 Mar., 29 Mar.
Lucky Days: 12 Mar, 24 Mar.
Misfortune Days: 11 Mar, 23 Mar.
Bad Days: 6 Mar, 8 Mar., 18 Mar., 20 Mar., 30 Mar.

Month 3 in the Snake Year (4 Apr 25 - 4 May 25)
This month, your horoscope will be a deadly line. When the evil power weakens your strength, your business will be full of obstacles

and problems. You must be careful about miscommunication that will bring problems. And relationships that are left behind will cause obstacles that will make your work not go smoothly. Your business will face storms. There will be conflicts within the organization and external disputes. Be careful not to be deceived when making long-term binding contracts.

What you should do during this period is to control yourself and not deviate from the path. Do your duties and responsibilities well. Be careful of protests or strikes in the organization. You should also be careful that your working capital will be affected by damages from debtors who are in arrears and become bad debts. You should also be careful not to use your emotions to respond to those who disturb you because if you respond strongly, it will be like pouring oil on the fire. Also, try not to interfere with other people's work or you will end up causing trouble for yourself unnecessarily. Starting work, investing, and investing during this period is not good.

Your finances this month will be in a state of losing money. Do not gamble or take risks. Do not do illegal business because you may not be able to escape criminal charges.

Your family is not peaceful. Be careful of unexpected silent dangers that will interfere with and cause anxiety in your home. You must be careful of losing valuables, being damaged, or falling victim to fraudsters. Relatives and friends should distance themselves from friends who often invite you to vices.

Health-wise, there will be problems during this period. Be careful of complications or infectious diseases and injuries from accidents.

In terms of love, you must be careful of arguing. Do not be selfish to the point of causing misunderstandings between each other. Do not meddle in other people's business and refrain from going to entertainment venues.

Support Days: 2 Apr., 6 Apr., 10 Apr., 14 Apr., 18 Apr., 22 Apr., 26 Apr., 30 Apr.
Lucky Days: 5 Apr., 17 Apr., 29 Apr.
Misfortune Days: 4 Apr., 16 Apr., 28 Apr.
Bad Days: 1 Apr., 11 Apr., 13 Apr., 23 Apr., 25 Apr.

Month 4 in the Snake Year (5 May 25 - 4 Jun 25)
This month, the horoscope of those born in the year of the Rooster will see the auspicious star shine, so it is a smooth and bright time to visit you again. As a result, the past obstacles will be resolved and improved. Storms and obstacles will gradually pass. Conflicts in work or business will have someone to help solve them. What you should do on this occasion is to look at your readiness and existing factors and then proceed according to the plan. You should also look for new investment channels or expand and build on the old ones. For starting a new job, investing in shares, and various investments, this month is a good opportunity for you to move forward. There will be openings that are worth investing in, and there

is a small chance of getting hurt. Therefore, you should seize them and not let them pass. In addition, during this period, you will find a sponsor for your work. Crises will be turned into opportunities. Therefore, you must increase your diligence and strengthen your knowledge because the more you do, the more money you will receive.

In terms of luck and finances, during this period, everything will flow smoothly, which will improve overall liquidity. However, you should not be careless. You still need to manage your income and expenses to be balanced throughout the year. Do not do anything that risks losing money unnecessarily.

In terms of family, it is still peaceful and smooth. During this period, you are likely to receive good news from people in your home. As for love, it is ripe. Those who are ready can walk hand in hand down the aisle of marriage. For those who have just found new love, even if you like it, you should take more time to study each other. For relatives and friends, this month you must be careful with your words because talking too much will bring problems. You also have to be careful of those who are two-faced and try to be close to you, hoping for benefits.

As for your health, there is nothing to worry about, but you should exercise and eat healthy food.

Support Days: 4 May, 8 May., 12 May., 16 May., 20 May., 24 May., 28 May.
Lucky Days: 11 May., 23 May.
Misfortune Days: 10 May., 22 May.
Bad Days: 5 May, 7 May, 17 May., 19 May., 29 May., 31 May.

Month 5 in the Snake Year (5 Jun 25 - 6 Jul 25)
This month, your horoscope will continue to improve from last month. The smooth energy will help your work or business find new opportunities or channels. This is another time

when you should increase your diligence, and diligently increase your new skills and knowledge. This will result in problems and obstacles accumulated from the previous month being resolved and resolved. Therefore, what you should do during this period is to increase your courage in investing or doing business. Then you will be successful, have more outstanding results than before, and be able to achieve your desired goals. You must also learn how to solve problems and manage systematically, adjusting long and short to achieve balance.

This month's finances are much better than last month. You will have a continuous inflow of money, both regular and special income. The more you work hard, the more results you will have or the opportunity to expand your income. Visiting customers and those you have to contact will help increase sales. Starting a new job, investing in shares, and various investments will find good opportunities.

A peaceful family horoscope will find supportive power. Relatives are the criteria for friends to help. You will receive new advice on how to deal with difficult problems, including good ideas.

In terms of love, it is in the position of the gods supporting you. Single Roosters have a chance to meet their right partner this month. Therefore, young men and women can look forward to it. Cupid is preparing to aim his arrow at the heart, wishing the couple success.

As for your health, you will be stronger during this period, but when traveling on the road, do not be careless. If sometimes you have to let a hot-headed person pass first, you must do so. This will reduce unnecessary problems and damage.

Support Days: 1 Jun., 5 Jun., 9 Jun., 13 Jun., 17 Jun., 21 Jun., 25 Jun., 29 Jun.
Lucky Days: 4 Jun., 16 Jun., 28 Jun.
Misfortune Days: 3 Jun., 15 Jun., 27 Jun.
Bad Days: 10 Jun., 12 Jun., 22 Jun., 24 Jun.

Month 6 in the Snake Year (7 Jul 25 - 6 Aug 25)
This month, the horoscope of those born in the year of the Rooster shows the auspicious stars moving into the horoscope house, causing the horoscope to be smooth and bright. Your career will be smooth. Businesses will find good sales and profits. During this month, there are things you should do: When your mind is clear, you may find time to explore the market to see the direction of change.

You should also find a way to initiate new things, revolutionize old things, and repeat rules and regulations that have slowed down your work. Increase your determination and diligence, and add new skills that will develop your work and business to a new path that will find better things than before.

During this time, your financial horoscope will be prominent. You will have direct and indirect cash flow, whether it be income from work successful work or good returns from financial supporters. In addition, you have a chance to invest in the business or purchase new assets or assets. However, you should manage your spending to balance with your income. If you spend too much until you forget yourself, there is a chance that your finances will be interrupted and have no liquidity. Starting a new job, investing in stocks, and various investments during this time have a bright direction.

Your family horoscope finds auspicious energy visiting you. This month, there are auspicious times for work, engagement, marriage, son's marriage, or daughter's marriage. Organize a birthday party or housewarming party, or for some, there may be a chance to welcome a new little member to the family.

Love without storms, singles have a good time to confess their feelings. For those who have a lover or partner, this period is sweet.

In terms of health, if there is an illness, it can be easily treated.

Support Days: 3 Jul., 7 Jul., 11 Jul., 15 Jul., 19 Jul., 23 Jul., 27 Jul., 31 Jul.
Lucky Days: 10 Jul., 22 Jul.
Misfortune Days: 9 Jul., 21 Jul.
Bad Days: 4 Jul., 6 Jul., 16 Jul., 18 Jul., 28 Jul., 30 Jul.

Month 7 in the Snake Year (7 Aug 25 -6 Sep 25)
This month, your horoscope will meet with auspicious power to support you, so you can soar. Both finances and work still have good opportunities, but you still need to take care of yourself because there are still lingering problems that have not yet been resolved. As for work and business, there will be progress. This month, no matter what work or business activities you plan to do, overall, it will be quite successful. Therefore, you should dare to move forward. There will be beautiful results. It is suitable for expanding work, increasing sales, and starting a new job. If you are ready, you should do it immediately. Strike while the fire is hot. What you should do during this period is to quickly solve the pending problems. You also

need to build and strengthen good relationships with people around you. Wait for a good opportunity to move forward again.

Your financial horoscope will have abundant income. You still have income from both regular salary and sales, as well as special income from additional work. Starting a new job, joint ventures, and various investments will be smooth during this period. However, if you hope to get money from gambling, be careful not to get hurt. Also, be careful not to fall into the trap of scammers because of greed.

The family is not good. You must be careful not to lose money because of subordinates due to unexpected events. In addition, you must take more care of the health of your family members.

For good physical health, you must always remember that "Don't drink and drive."

Your love life is still smooth and bright. This is a good time to take your loved one on a vacation or volunteer to help society and do good deeds together. This will help strengthen your love life in another way.

Support Days: 4 Aug., 8 Aug., 12 Aug., 16 Aug., 20 Aug., 24 Aug., 28 Aug.
Lucky Days: 3 Aug., 15 Aug., 27 Aug.
Misfortune Days: 2 Aug., 14 Aug., 26 Aug.
Bad Days: 9 Aug., 11 Aug., 21 Aug., 23 Aug.

Month 8 in the Snake Year (7 Sep 25 - 7 Oct 25)
This month, the life path of those born in the year of the Rooster is moving in a negative direction. Your destiny will fall dramatically, which will harm communication and negotiations. Business and trade agreements will be obstructed and not smooth. Business and trade will encounter obstacles. In addition, there will be unsmoothness in many aspects. Be careful with your words or manners that may

cause conflicts with your colleagues, which may create unnecessary problems. In terms of work, there will be conflicts. Be careful of people in the organization or outsiders who secretly harm or slander you. When making work contracts, be careful of hidden details that will put you at a disadvantage. The most important thing you should do during this period is to communicate clearly and be a good listener so that there will be no mistakes in your work.

In addition, you should be respectful of those who are older and try to build good relationships with people around you consistently. Otherwise, your work will not pass and you may have to work hard to fix it. To get through this crisis, you must stay calm and use your mind to lead in everything.

Your financial horoscope is not very good, so you should closely monitor your liquidity. Avoid extravagance. Do not gamble or invest in illegal or immoral businesses. Do not lend money and be a guarantor for anyone.

Including all investments, this period is not good. You should refrain from doing so for now.

As for the family horoscope, be careful of arguments and unexpected accidents in the house. Relatives and friends should still keep their distance to be safe from stray impacts.

In terms of love, there will be a storm. Be careful of anger without mindfulness. You will say hurtful words to your lover, which will cause a rift in your relationship.

In terms of health, be careful of injuries and bleeding from accidents, both while working and traveling.

Support Days: 1 Sep., 5 Sep., 9 Sep., 13 Sep., 17 Sep., 21 Sep., 25 Sep., 29 Sep.
Lucky Days: 8 Sep., 20 Sep.
Misfortune Days: 7 Sep., 19 Sep.
Bad Days: 2 Sep., 4 Sep., 14 Sep., 16 Sep., 26 Sep., 28 Sep.

Month 9 in the Snake Year (8 Oct 25 - 6 Nov 25)

This month, your horoscope is smooth and bright because many auspicious stars are orbiting into your horoscope house, so it shows a path of progress. This is a good opportunity for you to move forward and expand what is still pending. Those who work regularly should create more work. Those who do business should quickly increase sales and income because, during this period, you will find supporters. Therefore, you should quickly use this opportunity to make merit to enhance your charisma and horoscope to be even more prosperous.

In terms of work and business, even though there is progress during this period, you cannot trust those who do not wish you well in the organization and who will find an opportunity to harass, slander, or harm you. Therefore, your words and behavior during this period are another month that you should be careful. Do not act aggressively or look down on or insult others. Starting a new job, and entering into a joint venture, including various investments, during this period will have good results in return.

Your financial horoscope this month is quite good. Income comes from things you have invested and worked hard in. There is also a chance to receive extra money by taking a chance on the stock lottery.

In terms of love, this is a ripe time for those who do not dare to reveal their feelings and confess their love. This period is a good opportunity. However, for those who have a partner, the overall picture is still smooth as usual. But do not go to entertainment venues, there is a chance of getting sick and having problems later.

For a peaceful family, there is auspicious power visiting you. You have a chance of moving to a new place of residence, it may be a house change or a change of workplace. There is also a chance of buying expensive property into the house. There is also a chance of organizing an auspicious event.

In terms of health, even if there is an illness, it can be easily cured.

Support Days: 3 Oct., 7 Oct., 11 Oct., 15 Oct., 19 Oct., 23 Oct., 27 Oct., 31 Oct.
Lucky Days: 2 Oct., 14 Oct., 26 Oct.
Misfortune Days: 1 Oct., 13 Oct., 25 Oct.
Bad Days: 8 Oct., 10 Oct., 20 Oct., 22 Oct.

Month 10 in the Snake Year (7 Nov 25 - 6 Dec 25)
This month, your finances will be broken. There will be chaos in many matters. As for your work and business, this month you will face storms. You should be careful of changes in the market and products. In addition, your financial accounting system will have problems that will cause you concern. However, when faced with obstacles from all sides like this, you should plan to solve them in order of importance. Whatever will affect you in many areas, you must quickly resolve them and then solve other problems that are less important. As for investing in various businesses, this period is

not suitable. If you can postpone it, you should postpone it.

The most important thing you should do during this period is to take good care of your health and be careful of accidents. In terms of work, you should take care of your work as best you can. Do not interfere in other people's problems when you cannot survive.

In terms of your fortune and finances, you will be broken and lose your wealth. Therefore, you should prepare a backup plan, plan two or three, and closely manage your liquidity. Be careful of unexpected expenses. Do not gamble and take risks. Avoid investing large sums of money that are risky. Take care of and maintain your liquidity. Do not do illegal business because you may be imprisoned and fined.

In terms of family, there will be arguments. Therefore, you can compromise on anything that you can. When living under the same roof, you should take a step back, sacrifice, and share a little. Peace will come.

In terms of love, there will be conflicts that will not end easily. There will also be a third party that will disturb the relationship. You must be firm and calm. Avoid hanging out at entertainment venues.

In terms of health, you must be careful of high blood pressure from stress. Not getting enough rest will be the beginning of illnesses.
Support Days: 4 Nov., 8 Nov., 12 Nov., 16 Nov., 20 Nov., 24 Nov., 28 Nov.
Lucky Days: 7 Nov., 19 Nov.
Misfortune Days: 6 Nov., 18 Nov., 30 Nov.
Bad Days: 1 Nov., 3 Nov., 13 Nov., 15 Nov., 25 Nov., 27 Nov.

Month 11 in the Snake Year (7 Dec 25 - 4 Jan 26)
This month, your horoscope is falling from the normal line. Your career will encounter challenging obstacles. Businesses will face a test of your abilities. Storms and obstacles will strike from all sides. Therefore, you must analyze and assess the situation and find a way

to prepare for it well because problems will come continuously. If you assess that it is difficult to cope, you must try to maintain the original condition before thinking and doing anything else. Your career and business will be physically and mentally exhausted because your products may be attacked by competitors or become obsolete. Sales will drop. Therefore, you should plan to prevent the unevenness that will occur. What you should do this month is to focus and use your energy to the fullest. Study the root cause. Prepare to cope and always have a backup plan. Do not be careless and do not give up. In the encirclement, you will find a way out.

Your financial horoscope is falling, losing assets. Working capital will be stuck because income has decreased from sales that have decreased. Be careful not to leave debtor accounts for too long or you will get bad debts. What you can do is find a way to sell the remaining products and may need to ask for advice from experts with experience. Do not gamble, do not lend money, or sign as guarantors.

Do not invest in illegal businesses because if you make a mistake, you may think too much and become sick. Be careful not to be tricked when starting a new job, or investing in stocks and other investments.

This month, the family should face each other. Telling the truth is better than telling a lie. Relatives should distance themselves from friends who often invite them to vices.

As for love, it is easy to have arguments, so be careful not to interfere in other people's family matters and avoid going out at night.

In terms of health, you are likely to get sick. Be careful of liver disease and diabetes. You should find time to exercise and take care of your diet to build immunity.

Support Days: 2 Dec., 6 Dec., 10 Dec., 14 Dec., 18 Dec., 22 Dec., 26 Dec., 30 Dec.
Lucky Days: 1 Dec., 13 Dec., 25 Dec.

Misfortune Days: 12 Dec., 24 Dec.
Bad Days: 7 Dec., 9 Dec., 19 Dec., 21 Dec., 31 Dec.

Amulet for The Year of the Rooster
"The Four Guardian Deities holding a magical lute"

Those born in the year of the Rooster this year should set up and worship the sacred object "Lord Chatulokban Krong Phin Sret" to enhance their destiny. Place it on your work desk or cash desk to ask for his power and influence. It will help promote and increase auspicious things to have clear results, progress, and success, be filled with infinite fortune and wealth, have a peaceful and happy family, be filled with wealth, and have clear and complete wisdom and wisdom.

In one chapter of Advanced Feng Shui, it is mentioned about the deities who will come down to reside in the Mie Keng (the house of destiny) of the year, which are deities who can bring both good and bad things to the person of that year's destiny. Therefore, worshiping to enhance your destiny with the deity who comes down to reside in your birth year is considered to have the best results and have the most impact on you. This is to rely on the power of that deity to help protect you while your destiny is declining and having bad karma to alleviate it. At the same time, ask for his blessing to help inspire your business and trade to be smooth and as desired, and bring glory and prosperity to you and your family.

Those born in the year of the Rooster or Mie Keng (horoscope house) in the Iw sign, although this year is quite good for you, there are obstacles that you have to overcome. Those who do business will have more opportunities to develop and grow than those who are salaried employees. Overall, it will be a good opportunity to develop your career to have outstanding results and push your business to progress and see profits. However, because in your horoscope inauspicious stars are orbiting and harassing you, it will cause you to have conflicts and arguments with others easily. It will also cause you to suffer from misfortunes that you did not cause. Although this year is a year of progress in your career, business, and education, you will have difficulties with large expenses that are beyond expectations. You must be careful about health problems. In addition, you should control your words and try to avoid having problems and using emotions towards others.

In terms of love, it is suitable for those born in the year of the Rooster. Some couples are likely to agree to get married. However, in terms of health, you should stop working too hard and find time to rest for yourself.

If you want to solve or alleviate the misfortune, you should set up and worship "The Four Great Kings of the Four Heavenly Kings who hold the magic lute" to ask for their power and influence to help them dispel disasters and disasters, and to help those born in the year of the Rooster have smooth careers, successful businesses, and flowing wealth and fortune, and to have a peaceful and happy family as desired.

"Chi Kok Tian Wang" (or Thao Thatarat Maharaj) is considered one of the "Shi Tian Wang" (Xi Tai Tian Wang) or the Four Great Kings of the Four Heavenly Kings, who are the leaders of the Four Great Kings of the Heavens, which is the land of the gods that borders the human world. The four great gods act as the world guardians (protectors of the world) in the four major directions, with the duty of maintaining peace and order to support the righteous people who are steadfast in morality in both the human and divine worlds.

In addition, "The Four Great Kings of the Four Heavenly Kings" are also considered "Dharma guardians" or "Hu Huab", which are guardians of the Dharma or Buddhist religion, and are also guardians of various religious sites. In particular, their main duty is "Shikok Tianwang" (the great god of the lute) who was assigned by the Buddha to help protect all countries that believe in Buddhism to have peace and prosperity and to protect the religious sites of that country to be safe from all dangers. His appearance is dressed in armor like a great general, and one hand holds a four-stringed lute. Whenever Shikok Tianwang plays the lute, for countries that believe in Buddhism, the music that is heard will be a beautiful and soothing melody. But for any country that thinks of destroying the country of Buddhism, the music will turn into countless large fireballs that will fall from the sky. Therefore, he

"Shikok Tianwang" is a symbol of controlling the weather on earth. He is also a great god who helps people to be able to live smoothly in every aspect and achieve their goals. However, people who will receive convenience and success must be good and adhere to morality.

In addition, those born in the year of the Rooster should wear auspicious pendants in the shape of "Lord Chatulokpala holding a magical lute" hang around the neck or carry it with you when traveling near or far from home to make the person of destiny full of auspicious treasures, to have prosperity and progress in both business and trade, to have a peaceful and happy family throughout the year, to create better and faster efficiency and effectiveness than before.

Good Direction: Northeast, Southeast, and West
Bad Direction: East
Lucky Colors: Gold, Metallic, Yellow, White, and Silver.
Lucky Times: 7.00 – 08.59, 09.00 – 10.59, 17.00 – 18.59.
Bad Times: 05.00 – 06.59, 19.00 – 20.59., 23.00 – 00.59

Good Luck For 2025